Eternity Restoration Project

Eternity Restoration Project
new and selected poems

Kushal Poddar

HAWAKAL PUBLISHERS

Published by: **Hawakal Publishers**, 185, Kali Temple Road,
Nimta, Calcutta 700049, India.

Website: www.hawakal.com
Contact: info@hawakal.com

First edition: September, 2018

Printed and bound at *S. P. Communications,*
Kolkata

Cover Photograph: Anne Rydland
Cover Design: Bitan Chakraborty

ISBN-13: 978-93-87883-34-5

Price: INR 250/- [USD 9.99]

Pradnya Kushal

Contents

From *Scratches Within* 2016

Homebrewed Moonshine   11
Searching Around In F Minor   12
This Poem Is Not About The Serpent   13
Beloved She   14
Passive Rain   15
Moon   18
Father   19
Memory Like Water   20
Walk On The Water Project   21

From *Knowing Your Neighborhood* 2015

Shadows Have Their Lonely Ways   25
Reading In-between   27
Bruised Oranges   28

From *A Place For Your Ghost Animals* 2015

The Invertebrate   33
Burden   34
Unquestionable Love   35
Personal History Month   36
About The Black Cat   37
The Flight   38

Halloween   39
The Ghost Animals In Our Marriage   40
Moth   41

New Poems

Our Bodies of Water   45
Wilderness   46
Empty Infinity   47
Evening Market, East   48
Cadillac Tree, Alabama   49
Slow Diving   50
Need More Horsepower   51
Loving, Living   52
Hickey   53
Floodgates for The Other Kind   54
A No Good Looking Glass   55
Birds   56
The Edge   57
Owl   58
Gravity   59
Puppy   60
Grass Lives   61
Palm   62
Adam and Eve, Now   63
I'll Love To See You In A Summer Dress   64
Me Too   65
The Green House   66
The Hearth of the Heaven   67
Eternity Restoration Project   68

From *Scratches Within* 2016

Homebrewed Moonshine

You drag me across the water of our floor,
through the darkness of light sipping
through old Venetian blinds.

'There', you point at the drop of silver
on the dining table.

My OCD will mop it again and again,
and it will move from one spot to the following.
Our pet rabbit stares at me. It keeps
all the secrets of house-trapped moon.

Remember, once a pigeon came in?
You ran to switch off the fan, open the panes?
Till this night you believe you saved it.

Mop. Mop. Wipe.
The drop of light moves the time
from surface to face to surface to arm to water to darkness.

Searching Around In F Minor

My hand in yours,
my body tilts, stumbles
and follows you.

Whereto do you pull me?

I feel breathless.
What is it in this
empty room of monochrome
you want me to see?

I search around in F minor,
find nothing. Nothing,
is it the thing you want me to find?

This Poem Is Not About The Serpent

A serpent slimes its tiredness
to the end of hunger
and falls asleep midway.

I am the rodent,
pang inside the snake,

green beneath everything
looking for the second coming of rain.

Beloved She

My mother has a breathing island inside.
Choked stream all around.
At night leaves glow.

Inside her head a rain frog
seeks a tree to call for a higher mate.

Inside, my dead body seeks
the cold of dissection table.
My arms far stretched.
I am the God for autopsy.

Inside, the outdoor of our city
awaits for spring. Outside,
her inside blind-seeks for my eyes.

Passive Rain

1

Am I allowed to write
about you, rain?
If I can, will you let me
publish it?
Will thunder strike me?
Barrages crack and flood
the ankle of our attics?

2

The mad women
of our sky room
fight over a feather.

Leaves rain
within the rain,
and the bird
anchors its head
in its soft grey breast.

The mad women
call my name.
Come upstairs.
And if I shake my head
their world will quake.

3

I forgot the blue umbrella.
It's alright.

I did never buy it anyway.
Did I, from
the Das Brothers' shop closed for years?

'It's alright.'
You text. Enjoy
for both of us.

4

If I write about rain
will you get wet?
My paper boat cruises
towards your vortex.
Sinking remains foreseen.

5

Moon doesn't rise tonight.
Rain words sentence us
chorus of darkness.

You still wait to dine together?
I cannot promise I shan't
lose the track of home, time.
Again.

Fever rings for an answer.
The questions are not prepared.

Moon

My cousin's laughter leaps
from my uncle's fifth floor.
Moon muffles my scream.

On the cornice grows weeds of silence.
It cracks the code of bricks.
The crevice whistles when wind
journeys to the heart of the room.

You love moon, Mou? There is
no remedy for that. Sometimes
I breathe through my heart
and let my lungs pump out blood
through my nose.

Sometimes I know without seeing
how you stoop to mop the red
and instead pick up the pieces
of moonshine from the floor.

Father

Noon zeroes all roads
towards one mango tree shade.

You know, I keep
a hive inside my skull.
I name each bee carefully.
You know their squad
is meant for suicide.
My nerve ends eye their stings.
Their stings observe
my pre-blindness.

Last time I met my father
he had the blueprint of me
that he folded and refolded
into a sperm and inserted
inside my mother.
I hope they read the letter I am.

Memory Like Water

Did I ever feel water?
One night I drowned
my mind in a glass of cold.
Bubbles. Bubbles.
And then, nothing more.

Water has a memory,
you know, and a central system
for processing bites.
I wonder if it remember
all those dead fish.

The other day I went
to an island in Far East.
No one goes there,
stays for a night.
The fright strolls on the shore
and unlocks the door
to the back forest.

After it leaves hope takes its place.
If you survive that
you are blessed.

Walk On The Water Project

Day One

A leaf is an island.
All of them are.

From the island of an ant
the shaft of light
saunters to the tiny spider island.

I should have left the pier.
I have no one to bid goodbye.

Day Two

Your feather
has a lonely body.

Its monochrome journey
reaches the spot of rainbow.

My toes test the water.
Skin tastes its pristine cold.

Day Three

Imagined you standing
in the middle lake.

Every step I take
sinks me a little.

Every step takes me back
to the beginning of the end.

Day Four

The birds circle my wet hair.
Water cascades from my body.

Breathing tires me.
Air burns my lungs.

I surface- the words
from an unspoken dream-

my feet speeds towards the blue,
albeit everything is azure.

Everything is calm.
When the lake grin
its skin creases into a thousand wrinkles.

From *Knowing Your Neighborhood* 2015

Shadows Have Their Lonely Ways

You have grown old for
sneaking up from behind,
shadow.

The fall burns my knees,
my palms. I desire
to run

back to noon and
unleash the full sun,
but I

know- we, old mates should
laugh off all rages.
Oh, you

so good at this game.
The moment I turn
you creep

behind me again
and again. The pine
whose hand

touched the rose bush now
enters into the barn.
A soft

owl screeches low over,
and an echo shapes
mother,

calling from our old
detached dwelling.

Reading In-between

This must be about your mother,
I say reading a sad piece.
No, the poet shakes his head, *I
wrote about the day I first
visited the circus.* I nod.
The same thing. A lioness
leaps through a flaming ring into
my mind. They kept her hungry
all day, promised to let her see
her cub after she marvels
at this trick, and they whispered
in my ear- Be her cub, she won't
know the difference. *This, a sad
song,* I say. *No, about
a fun day,* says the poet.

Bruised Oranges

He gives away
bruised oranges.

Back in our
mother's kitchen

we part the good
from the bad

and bad from worse,
and sometimes

they stick to
each other,

hold truths back,
hide their nectar,

roll in the drain-
gutted, gleaming.

Nearby stands
the center

for halfway back
all girl convicts,

we call- Afterlife,
but sometimes

oranges are just
oranges.

From *A Place For Your Ghost Animals* 2015

The Invertebrate

Do not mix your moth and your fire.
Turn your glass to cage its flutter.

The ceiling fan chops the stillness
in air that becomes the wind, breeze.

Rust on rust, gurgles the tab. I
hear a muffled scream in its stream.

Later, a choked invertebrate
shows up between the basin's teeth.

I shall release you, moth. I shall
stand on my peeling-away porch

and see you wave back. Oh such joy.
Can I afford to bear it? Your

freedom depends on the answer.

Burden

I paid for your trouble,
says the girl from the brothel

when you gasp for breath,
and on your tongue rolls

the taste of sea, and all you see
turns blurry. So you hear

the calmness of the girl,
Take back your husband.

He finished his bargain.
Now his sin is yours.

Unquestionable Love

I do not question
my friend's love-life, fear
it will elongate
our coffee-break, know
she can embrace the world,
has a place in her
two a.m. sudden
awakenings for
all of us, even
our cats, dogs and birds
who count her sleepy
dives of eyelids.
She says, anyway,
her love appears
as a void outlined
by the flight of white ants.
I sip my coffee.
All black inside
a rim of white.

Personal History Month

The death of the tomatoes falls on the wedding week.
They served good fish amidst
the whisper, "the caterer
mixed up the menu with
a funeral in next plot."
She drives back thinking about
the vow, years ago, to have
a double wedding,
the craze those days. She drives hard.
Tired back. Stands before the light
from her daughter's door. A note
on the refrigerator
proclaims Personal History Month.
Don't cry, old friend. I cannot
fathom what you say over
the telephone.

About The Black Cat

The window has no cat on its sill,
in its frame. Not even those dark ones
we pretend are invisible. No.
It shows a thick patch of black between
two lamps. No black cat. The rag coils in
oblivion. The woman who slept
for the last time when the towers fell,
exhausted, bereft of any sense,
sits half-lit on the couch where the cat
should have been practicing winter. No.
No cat. But I tell you brother, this
entire scene is a cat. A black cat.

The Flight

Please turn off your electronic instruments.
You leave the ground. The city flickers into
its fairer self. Then comes the kite. A black kite
with a red tail that wobbles inside the clouds.
You see nothing, but a string flies it for the boy
who stole an hour from his job, from his shanty
behind the runway and ran away with his kite.
It flies higher than our craft and still stays below.
Sir, please enjoy this flight that remains tethered
to its origin, a city built with mud,
yellow river and flesh.

Halloween

Today we make fun of a pumpkin
the way we see those kids do it in
another land. You left the lamp close
to the curtains. An easy way to
celebrate the fear we nurse for years,
that we shall have no home.
"Remember Sen?" You ask. Yes. His parents halved
him.
Now both kill each other. One from the head.
The other from the tail. You say, what better
way to end a fear than to have it here?
Forgive me, brother. I extinguish
the blaze. I lied even about our parents.
We must live them out. Be frightened. Witness
them beating each other for blood, bear
the shadow of love through their veins.

The Ghost Animals In Our Marriage

I place some ghost animals
on the desert around. We
landscaped the space, spent nights, days
on the proper emptiness.
I never asked you if I
could release those beasts whose eyes
I wished you would see on our
anniversary and shake.
They begin to ding. Do you
like them? See, if you connect
the ones on the east they will
form a tiger that died this morning
so I can make love and war.
If you connect those in the west,
they become the bison in
whose eyeholes live the purest tribes.
Do you like them, Hon? Will you
hike with me down the desert
where our songs tumble, roll, and
one spark causes a sustained blaze?

Moth

The shadow belongs to a moth
fluttering against the October walls.
You show me how a change in light
can make its wings the theatrics of your hands
pinned to your wrists, to your blades, to
the back of your heart that flies too near
a fire after each rain.

New Poems

Our Bodies of Water

In the summer pond
we dot night's monochrome.

Your finger stills a ripple.
Somewhere the city is a scratch on the silence.

Moon skinny-dips
and swims near our crotches.
If I open my mouth my tongue will fly out with a hoot.

Wilderness

My mind giraffes
into your mind.
Your soul wears a zebra today.

My peaceful lioness
waits beneath a baobab.
Soon you will dare
to quench your thirst.

Empty Infinity

The afternoon sun
strokes the hair
of the beggar-man
dead since this morning.

I feel jealous.

Four directions
place houses and trees
on the chessboard of the city.

No one else is alive.

Evening Market, East

New moon rests
in the summery cold.
Harvests bunch up
in the evening-fold.
So much rebirth, tiredness,
grains, sweat.
Let the dead girl float up
and sigh put some clouds.
Below, the market of faces
barters in expressions.
Late as it is,
everything sells cheap.

Cadillac Tree, Alabama

A tree wakes up
inside an abandoned Cadillac.
My devil tongue
pours a plan into its roots
to ride together
to the East, West, North and South
of everything.
My hand touches its skin.
It is so Art Deco.
It is the giddy youth
growing up in a town of no one else.
Let's go for ride, I say.
Sky of long roads wakes up
inside the bonnet of my chest.

Slow Diving

A slow diving
arrowhead bird
almost catches
the grey tail of a fish.

The music
of a horse turning in the meadow
echoes through the midday.
I inhale sun, sigh out my shade.

Need More Horsepower

Everything made of water
freezes into the shape and size
I felt them the last time.

Means, I wake up.

From the power stable of my soul
morning brings out more horses,
muscles, flesh.

Means, I wake up.

My hands press the balcony
down to the ground.
Sky is full of incoherent feathers.

I wake up. I mean it.

Loving, Living

You give me
all those years you lived
before meeting me
one evening amidst
birdcalls and sundown.

I gift you
all those I lived through.

"Where shall we keep these?"
You ask without moving your lips.

We turn towards the dinghy
afloat near the end of knowing,
its boatman feeling
nothing anymore.

We both know.

Hickey

My teeth dredge out
an island
on the estuary of your neck-
a delta between
the rising ray of a smile
and the broad strokes of your flesh,
brine at its best,
beads of salt rainbows all over its spread.

My teeth move again.
They will reach your soul soon,
near the hour of the crows.
Tonight breeze tests
the shelf life of our mosquito net.
Its threads croon for
the lost crew of an old fishing boat.

Floodgates for The Other Kind

Flood came in July.
Juliet, nothing
worked except
a boat-makeshift
crafted by
the out of work mailman.
Juliet, I rode in
 the love-note paper canoe,
felt- I was Noah
and if we should ever meet
we should spread
the religion of mails.
The red head letterbox
would be the new temple
whose turret light would kiss
the first thing in the morning.
Flood came in July, Juliet.
Can you hear my presence?

A No Good Looking Glass

You ask about the mirror's position.
All do. Why does one have a mirror
far above the reach of any reflection?
I know not.
Sometimes I dream of an eye on my wall.
It sees, shows nothing.
Sometimes a folk of pink flamingoes
fly out of its dusty gloss.
Sometimes my shadow climbs up,
crawls through it, seeks the Eden of wet thoughts.

Birds

Today the sorrow didn't come.
I waited for its swash,
minuscule footmarks.
I miss its steady hungry urgent chirping.

I take all my feeds back home.
A wonderful life, I sing.

The Edge

Once I find my mother
in her room
cornered by silence-

The still white of an owl hovers
in the air laden with pre winter.
From our roof
one sees mist and more mist.

And those long eyes of clouds
writhe for my gravity.

Owl

Through the mist
the hoots of an owl
reach for our sleep.

In this forest
once we rode facing the rear
of the same bareback nightmare.

Now we joyride.

The softness of an owl's flight
schedules night.
Everything is on time.

In this forest we
we buried our kaput dolls once.
Thickness of shrubs grows over time.

Now we play house.

Gravity

The same string
holding the lone star
in the thatched sky

pulls me in
and keeps me distant.

Oh you.
Oh me.
Oh ocean.

Puppy

Somewhere
a mass grave of stars exists.
There silence stands still
leaning against time's shovel.

I told these to my aunt
burst burying her fifth puppy.

Grass Lives

My parents
outsourced their wishes.
I live on the grass
grown in the space in between.

Once I saw a snake
wiggling through this land.
Once I saw Eve stripping all her Prada.

Palm

A dot of ink dashes down the white.
Night. Arctic. Silence piles up a hill.

All these you see on my palms?
Instead of lines? Instead of some star-shades?

All gloaming, once you leave
I lower my face on them to melt the permafrost.

Adam and Eve, Now

Strip, strip down from limo to tricycle
to four legged crawl.
Adam and Eve now. No one
whispers knowledge.
No text, subtext. Today I name
a bird a bird. You love. Myself I.
Eyes stare at the naked bead
on the blades of grass,
and so many colors frighten us.

So many colors conceive us.
Your finger is the first love letter.
Tomorrow we shall invent home
and slice a piece of eternity off the entirety.
Today, we are Adam and Even,
and my lips experience earthquake.
Unlearning silence seems so hard.

I'll Love To See You In A Summer Dress

Summer dress
blows over your head,
upstream wind,
shoreside crabs
nibbling nerve ends,
a bird on its one leg,
its wings halfway undone.
Salt sniffs your skin for sweat.
Summer dress, off white,
creased rustling unravels
to some notes of whim.

Me Too

endured the guilt of measuring
a princess
by the index of the comfort of a pea

while believing
a tradition means only a few
hundred years' of practice.

I too wore
the skin of a big bad wolf
pretending it is for the months of white

while
you, Goddess, bled,
and your red rode down ahead.

The Green House

The green flashbulbs of the trees
greet our heads tilted upwards.
Suspire. We knew this word.

We knew this word. Now suspire.
My fingers breathe the skin,
and within the lean veins streams touch.

Why are we searching for an address here?
Stop. This forest is the address in barks.

The Hearth of the Heaven

A man with divine limbs
pushes his
wheelchair across the B.T. Road.

A slant shaft of ray
reveals his legs for a jiffy,
and then they became clouded.

The wings a crow
take it home via a few dustbins.
Soon the wife, a puckeroo lady,

opens the gate and greets
the man to his heaven.
The world is still in the oven.

Eternity Restoration Project

Planks of light build a house,
another, another,
and a colony is built.
Windows breathe.
Two children freeze a ball
in between them.
All night the boy pasted posters
on every wall-
Soon. Eternity is coming.

Acknowledgments

Those who added flesh to my soul and published some of my significant works before- David McCoy and Spare Change Press, Julie Kim Shavin, Bill Young , Ripple Effect Publications LLC, Valli Poole and BRP Australia, Barbara Maat and Andrew Bellon, Franz Wright, Chris Madoch, Zachary Guadamour, Duane Vorhees, Reuben Woolley, Donna Snyder, my wife Pradnya Kushal and all of my friends and especially my critics.